Implementing Student Self Assessment

David Boud
University of Technology, Sydney

HERDSA

HERDSA Green Guides

Series Editor:

Vic Beasley, Language and Learning Unit, The Flinders University of South Australia

Editorial Committee:

Robert Cannon, The University of Adelaide
Gerry Mulins, The University of Adelaide
Marie Williamson, University of South Australia
Peter Younger, University of South Australia

Published by
Higher Education Research and Development Society of Australasia Incorporated
c/- PROBLARC, PO Box 555, Campbelltown, NSW, Australia 2560

National Library of Australia
Cataloguing-in Publication data

Boud, D.J. (David J.).
    Implementing student self-assessment.

    2nd ed.
    Bibliography
    ISBN 0 908557 19 1.

    1. Students - Self-rating of. I. Higher Education Research and Development Society of Australasia. II. Title. (Series: HERDSA green guide; no. 5).

378.167

The Author

David Boud is Professor of Adult Education at the University of Technology, Sydney. Prior to that he was Professor and founding Director of the Professional Development Centre, University of New South Wales.

Contents

Foreword

In his report for the Commonwealth Tertiary Education Commission, *Academic Development Units*, Professor Richard Johnson said, in reference to knowledge about educational matters:

> There exists a substantial body of knowledge on many of these matters and there are techniques for finding answers to the questions. However, just because the body of knowledge is substantial, just because the processes of higher education are complex, it cannot be expected that the academic pursuing research and teaching in another discipline or the administrator coping with the day-to-day and year-to-year urgencies of an institution can master or keep up with the range of contemporary thinking and research results.

While that is certainly correct it is also true that most staff in tertiary education are interested in carrying out their various tasks and responsibilities well.

To this end many of them would appreciate some guidance on one or other of these tasks and responsibilities. But staff do not have time for a detailed study of the literature on these issues. The other reason for the frustration of staff who go in search for guidance is that many of the publications available are written by people who are conscious of the academic tradition of writing and hence prepare treatises that attempt to be comprehensive, argued in detail and fully documented. This is not what staff need — they need some ideas and pointers that they can relate to their particular circumstances and some brief guidance to further reading if they so desire.

The publications in this HERDSA Green Guide Series are explicitly designed to meet these needs. They are relatively short, inexpensive, easy to read, and concentrate on supplying ideas rather than a fully argued comprehensive cover of an area. Their bibliographies are deliberately not comprehensive but are designed to be helpful — these are *not* academic studies of an area but, as the series title indicates, guides.

Each Guide is designed to cover one aspect of a staff member's tasks and responsibilities. Each Guide has been commissioned by the HERDSA Publications Committee and refereed but the content is the responsibility of the particular author(s) and does not necessarily represent the views of the Committee or the Society.

We hope that staff will find the Guides useful and welcome comments on individual Guides and on other areas that could be covered by similar volumes.

HERDSA Publications Committee

Introduction

Self assessment involves students taking responsibility for monitoring and making judgements about aspects of their own learning. Some students are effective in making self assessments and engage in this activity as part of their normal study patterns. Other students are less naturally self-reflective or have not developed the appropriate skills earlier in their career. All students, whether they are familiar with self assessment or not, need to consider how they can monitor their own performance when confronted with new types of knowledge and skills.

Self assessment requires students to think critically about what they are learning, to identify appropriate standards of performance and to apply them to their own work. Self assessment encourages students to look to themselves and to other sources to determine what criteria should be used in judging their work rather than being dependent solely on their teachers or other authorities. The development of skills in self assessment lies at the core of higher education, and as teachers we should be finding whatever opportunities we can to promote self assessment in the courses we teach.

Self assessment is much more than the allocation of grades. It is as much a learning activity as an assessment activity. Indeed, in many cases it is entirely separate from the formal assessment of students. It may take place as an exercise alongside other course requirements or it may be linked to formal assessment procedures.

Self assessment is a term which describes a very wide range of practices some of which are more defensible as a part of higher education than others. It is important that one's view of what is valuable in self assessment is not coloured by the sometimes disreputable practices of the past. The laissez faire approach adopted by a few in the 1970s when students were encouraged to award themselves whatever grade they chose has proved an inhibition on staff thinking about self assessment, obscuring more recent developments which are exploring the value and effectiveness of rather more systematic approaches.

The importance of self assessment in higher education can perhaps be indicated by reference to a major survey of graduates of the University of New South Wales carried out in 1983 by Midgley and Petty on behalf of the Alumni Association. Responses were obtained from 1842 graduates across a variety of disciplines. In a question concerning the skills a university education might be expected to develop, respondents rated the importance of each skill and indicated the extent to which their own undergraduate education had contributed to the acquisition of these skills. The results were:

	Extent of the university's contribution to their acquisition		
Skills required by graduates (in order of graduates rating of importance):	Considerable	Some	Little
1. Solving problems	58%	35%	6%
2. **Evaluating one's own work**	**20**	**53**	**27**
3. Written communication and report writing	36	47	17
4. Ability to work in a team	20	42	38
5. Managerial skills	5	19	76
6. Oral presentation	10	38	52
7. Information retrieval	35	44	20
8. Evaluating the work of others	13	34	53
9. Computing skills	20	34	46

Ratings by University of New South Wales alumni of skills required by graduates (n=1842)
Source: Midgley and Petty 1983

Graduates rated the ability to evaluate their own work very highly, but only 20% felt that the contribution of the university to the achievement of this goal was 'considerable' while 27% thought that the university's contribution to it was 'little'. Graduates seemed to have no doubt that self assessment was an important skill, but they also believed that the university generally had contributed less than it might have towards development of that skill.

The aim of this guide is to examine the role of self-assessment in courses in higher education and to provide assistance to those who wish to use self-assessment in courses they teach. It draws on the experience of staff in different disciplines who developed and evaluated forms of self-assessment which were suited to many different conditions: class size, subject matter, teaching approach, and available time. The ideas presented here have been tested with participants in a number of workshops and seminars which have been conducted to disseminate the findings of the research and in development work conducted in collaboration with colleagues in different disciplines.

Following a brief account of the background to self assessment, the idea of self assessment is discussed and some of the implications for teachers in introducing it are examined. Key issues in self assessment are mentioned and the process is illustrated by six case studies of the application of self assessment practices in undergraduate courses.

Brief Background and History

Some work on student self-assessment was reported as early as the 1930s, much of it based in the US, but most reported research up until the late 1960s was concerned with comparisons between the grades generated by students and those generated by their instructors. In summary, with some exceptions, this kind of research has found that students were able to predict the grades they would be given with reasonable accuracy (Boud and Falchikov 1989, Falchikov and Boud 1989). Students in introductory courses and in earlier years of their programmes tended to slightly overrate themselves, whereas students in advanced courses and later years tended to slightly underrate themselves. Many of these studies were not rigorously designed, and it was common, for example, for it not to be reported clearly whether or not the grades generated were to form part of a formal assessment. The results should therefore be treated cautiously.

Interest in other aspects of self-assessment increased in the early 1970s, especially in professional schools in medicine and teacher education, and a shift of emphasis occurred towards developing ways in which students and practitioners could appraise their own work. Concern with grading still existed, but other more fundamental educational issues began to be examined. Studies were less concerned with the predictability of students' ratings than with engaging students in activities which related to their future professional tasks.

At that time the involvement of students' peers in assessment featured more strongly than self assessment as such, perhaps in response to the peer review movement which had begun to be established in medicine. Studies comparing grades or marks have continued to appear until the present day in a number of subjects: education, dietetics, guidance and counselling, psychology, liberal arts, social sciences, law and others as well. Unfortunately, there have been no major investigations which aim to systematically identify what factors influence the grades students will give themselves. However, it is clear that the grading practices of teachers and the extent to which students are competing with each other for grades are important.

The late 1970s saw a general recognition of the educational value of self assessment – something which has been stressed by a great many authors over the last decade. There were related developments in the areas of grade contracting where students contract with a teacher to produce an assignment for a particular grade which is then assessed as satisfactory or unsatisfactory, and also in self-testing where students complete multiple-choice tests which they mark themselves. The latter area has been subjected to much research at the Open University (Gale 1984).

In the mid-1970s considerable impetus was given by Heron's conceptual work, and its subsequent development (Heron 1988). Heron was working in the context of professional development and experiential learning. He provided a clear rationale for self assessment based on the importance of learners accepting responsibility for their learning and on the need for the development of self assessment skills for professional life (Heron 1981). He also stressed the fundamental importance of self assessment to learning and discussed the valuable role peers can play in self assessments.

More recent work by the present author and collaborators has attempted to extend previous research and development on self assessment into new areas such as engineering (Boud and Holmes 1981, Boud, Churches and Smith 1986), law (Boud and Tyree 1980), science education (Boud and Prosser 1980), architecture (Boud and Lublin 1983), university teaching (Boud and Kilty 1985), distance education (Boud 1981) and postgraduate coursework (Boud, forthcoming). For references to particular literature in this historical development, readers are referred to an annotated bibliography which is obtainable from the author. Much of the work which has been published describes particular forms of self-assessment in particular courses and there is relatively little cross-referencing by authors.

What is self assessment?

The defining characteristic of self assessment is the involvement of students in:

>   identifying standards and/or criteria to apply to their work and

>   making judgements about the extent to which they have met these criteria and standards.

Students should be involved in making decisions on the basis of various kinds of information. some of this they may generate themselves, other data may derive from teachers, practitioners and peers. Self assessment does not imply that students work in isolation from the views and judgements of others.

Self assessment is commonly a supplement to teacher assessment of students, although in some cases it may replace it. Teachers have an important part to play in student assessment; however, if they see themselves as the only assessors they can limit the achievement of many of the central goals of higher education. Many existing assessment practices can encourage an inappropriate dependency by students on staff. The danger of an excessive reliance on teacher assessment is that students learn to look to their teachers and distrust their own assessments. They may be inhibited in becoming independent learners who can exercise their own critical judgement. Self assessment is not just another technique for testing student achievement. It is a way for students to become involved in assessing their own performance. In this process they may in fact use quite familiar and routine techniques which differ little or at all from those regularly used by teachers for testing achievement. The ends to which these methods are put characterise self assessment.

Self assessment means more than students grading their own work; it means involving them in the processes of determining what is good work in any given situation. They are required to consider what are the characteristics of, say, a good essay or practical report and to apply this to their own work.

Can students be effectively involved in both stages of the assessment process: determining criteria and making judgements? The answer to this important question seems to be both 'yes' and 'no'. There do exist some subjects of either a highly technical or conceptually sophisticated nature in which it may not be practically possible at introductory levels to involve students in the specification of criteria. However, while students may not be able to articulate criteria as such at this stage, they can often recognise the applicability of criteria provided by others.

In such cases as these, where students use only the criteria provided by staff the term "self-marking" or "self-testing" is used rather than "self assessment". There is, however, some confusion on this point in the literature and it is common to find, especially in work emanating from the Open University, people using 'self assessment' to describe the very limited notion of student-marked tests (e.g., Gale 1984).

CASE STUDY 1:   Self and peer marking in an electrical engineering examination.

This study investigated the limited notion of student self-marking with a third year undergraduate class of over one hundred students studying electronic circuits at the University of New South Wales. Students were involved in assessing their own performance and that of one of each of their peers in a mid-semester examination.

As an alternative to the normal marking procedure for this examination, students received detailed model answers and commentaries with which they could compare their own solutions – or those of their peers – in the completed examination papers and thus allocate marks.

At the first class meeting after the examination each was randomly allocated the unnamed paper of one other student in the class. They marked this in their own time using the model answers and marking schedule.

They were required to indicate in detail on a marking sheet exactly where the other student had departed from the model solution and to award a score for each section on a scale provided. They returned the papers and marking sheets the following week and received their own examination script.

They then applied the same procedure to their own paper without knowing what marks might have already been awarded it by someone else. The self and peer generated marks for the examination were then compared, and if percentage marks were within 10% of each other then the student was awarded the self-mark. In cases of greater discrepancy than 10%, the paper was re-marked by a staff member. In order to discourage students colluding with each other to fix marks to maximise their grade (which had earlier been identified as a potential problem) other papers were sampled at random by staff.

A procedure for administering this scheme was evolved over four successive semesters to minimise staff time, to ensure equitable distribution of papers, and to minimise collusion in mark-fixing. Student response was positive and staff reported that there was a considerable saving in staff marking time, even allowing for the increase in time in preparing model answers and organizing the movement of papers. The saving was calculated to be greater the larger the number of students enrolled in the class.

This study also showed that it is possible to develop a self marking procedure which is acceptable to both staff and students. The crucial condition is that the scheme be progressively modified to address at least some of the problems and deficiencies which inevitably occur when any scheme of this type is introduced.

Details of this study appear in Boud and Holmes (1981). Minor modifications to the procedure have since led to a higher level of acceptance by students than the already high earlier level. There has also been a decrease in the concern expressed about collusion. The method has been incorporated into the course as a regular feature since the first trial in 1978, and a variation of the method has been adopted by another staff member in the same School independently of the researchers. In 1983 the procedure was modified by using tutorial time for self and peer marking, as it was possible to complete the whole marking process within a one hour tutorial period.

However, while accepting the usefulness of self-marking as described in Case Study 1, the main thrust of this Guide looks to a possible involvement of students in *both* the stages we have specified above – identifying criteria and making judgements – to the extent that the subject itself, and other circumstances, may permit.

Premises

The theory and practice of self assessment is based on several premises about the development of students.

1. Self assessment is a necessary skill which should be developed by all students

It is important for students to develop the ability to be realistic judges of their own performance and to effectively monitor their own learning. Graduates who develop the skill are more likely to:
- wish to continue their learning,
- know how to do so,
- monitor their own performance without constant reference to fellow professionals, and
- expect to take full responsibility for their actions and judgements.

2. Self assessment needs to be developed in undergraduate courses.

It is appropriate to develop this skill as part of tertiary courses. Its development represents one of the most important processes that can occur in undergraduate education. If students are to be able to continue learning effectively after graduation and make a significant contribution in their own professional work, they must develop skills of appraising their own achievements during their student years. The foundation for this should occur at the undergraduate level if not earlier.

Self assessment is not an isolated activity which can be practised independently of the courses which students study. It should find its way, to a greater or lesser extent, into all courses: the requirements for monitoring performance can differ from one area of knowledge to another.

3. Self assessment is necessary for effective learning.

The third premise is even broader and is one which forms a particularly important part of the thinking of those who are committed to such goals as autonomy or independence in learning. It is that, for effective learning of any kind to take place at any stage, learners – whoever they may be – must develop the capability of monitoring what they do and modifying their learning strategy appropriately.

Effective learning also involves learners being able to influence their own learning rather than waiting for others to do so. Those who require the impetus of others, be they teachers or supervisors, to develop and assess their knowledge and skills are severely handicapped in their learning.

The effect of students' undertaking assessment of their own work is suggested by the improvement in the product of their learning described in Case Study 2.

CASE STUDY 2:   Class generated criteria for self assessment in a law research assignment.

It was decided to investigate the use of a common set of criteria which had been agreed by a group of students; hence it became necessary to find ways for students to generate and negotiate criteria as a group.

The study was begun in a later year subject (International Trade Law) at the University of New South Wales, and an additional subject (Law of Banking) was subsequently included. The process involved students taking part in a meeting at which they presented individual criteria and then reached consensus on a common set of criteria using a nominal group approach (see page ??).

They then used these criteria to assess a major research assignment. This involved making a detailed critique of their own assignment with respect to these criteria and submitting this at the same time as their assignment itself. The self assessment was contained in a sealed envelope and not seen by the staff member until the assignment had been marked. Students were asked to give themselves a grade, but this was not used for assessment purposes.

Of the fifteen students over two years who completed the research option, all completed the self assessment, and the most striking outcome was that the staff member observed a clear, qualitative improvement in assignment work relative to previous years when self assessment was not used. Although the criteria setting and negotiating session took one and a half hours from a normal class, the staff member and students alike regarded it as time well spent.

Strategies for Implementation

How can we teach students to assess themselves? In this section some ways to introduce self assessment and procedures which can be used both for individuals and for groups are discussed. Some pitfalls to avoid are also indicated.

Who gets the ball rolling – and how?

The idea of self assessment may, in principle, be introduced by either staff or students. In practice, however, it is more likely that staff will take the initiative. whoever introduces the idea, it will normally be necessary for them to:
- give the rationale for its introduction,
- explain how it is to operate,
- and clearly identify the purposes to which it will be put.

The rationale for its introduction most frequently concerns improved learning and the development of self assessment skills. If this is the case then it is appropriate to introduce the process as a component of the regular teaching and learning activity rather than as an element of the formal assessment procedure.

Gauge student attitudes

Students need to be at least neutral or – most preferably – sympathetic towards the purposes of self assessment, in order to introduce it. There are two issues to contend with:

Firstly, acceptance versus hostility.

Because one of the prime aims of self assessment is to actively engage students in thinking critically about their own learning, it is necessary for them to see at least some worth or value in the particular form of self assessment to which they are introduced. The problem is that in many contexts its value is not immediately self evident. To a significant degree, the views of students are influenced by staff and by the overall institutional or departmental milieu. They bring with them a great many attitudes formed during their earlier experiences of learning. The effect of each of these factors can be either supportive or hostile to the idea of self-assessment.

Secondly, learning styles and motivations.

In professional courses it is not unusual for students to adopt a strictly instrumental approach towards learning. They see their task to be that of satisfying the sometimes mysterious requirements of the teaching staff. When this is encountered it can only be met by resort to instrumental arguments, such as: "this will lead to better grades", if this is true and likely to be the case, or else "this is part of the course requirements". The positive experience of student self assessment in similar courses can also be reported.

Case Study 3 provides an example of some of the motivation problems which can be encountered in self assessment in a professional course.

CASE STUDY 3:   Self assessment with peer feedback in an architectural design project.

A reasonable expectation regarding final year courses, and particularly those involving project work, is that students would have a reasonably sophisticated view of the criteria which should apply to their own work. We have found, however, that they often have not had enough experience to develop these criteria and to apply them in an objective way.

They may also benefit greatly by being given alternative view points from which to consider their work. These alternative viewpoints can be provided by staff, but it can sometimes be difficult for students not to feel obliged to conform to staff views when staff are the ultimate assessors. In this case peers are a useful source of ideas and opinions which can be fed into the self assessment process and help inform the perspective of students.

It was considerations such as these that prompted this study in a final year design subject in the School of Landscape Architecture at the University of New South Wales. A few weeks after receiving a design brief students were asked to determine individually the criteria which they considered should be applied to judging the outcomes of the design project. They were asked to include both general considerations of good design and those factors which were unique to the particular problem which had been set.

When projects were completed, the 16 students met for a
one day session. They viewed each others' designs and
gave and received feedback. The format for this day was
to display designs in the morning, then have opportunity
to look at each one at leisure. In the afternoon each would
receive feedback from the others during a peer feedback
session in which ten minutes were allocated per student.
Guidelines were provided on ways to give and receive
useful feedback (see Appendix).

Following this session students completed a self
assessment of their own project. The criteria used were
those originally chosen, but modified in the light of both
their own experience and that of the feedback from their
peers. The outcomes did not form part of the formal
assessment system. There was also a degree of student
attrition during the process, and only eleven of the original
sixteen completed the self assessment.

There were a number of factors outside this particular
activity which contributed to difficulties in completing
the study. However there was evidence from those
students who did complete the final evaluation that they
had found the exercise productive. In addition, many
suggestions were made about how elements of the self
assessment activity and particularly the peer feedback
session should be incorporated as a normal part of the
course.

'Selling' the idea

If it is assumed that students have had their main initial concerns
satisfactorily addressed, the next step is for them to experience a
process which has some sort of face validity for them. The requirements
for this appear to be:
- a clear rationale; what are the purposes of this particular
  activity?
- explicit procedures; students need to be clear about what is
  expected of them,
- reassurance; of a safe environment in which they can be honest
  about their own performance without the fear that they will
  expose information which can be used against them,
- confidence; that others will do likewise, and that in the case of
  peer assessment cheating or collusion will be detected and
  discouraged.

Timing: choosing the best stage for introduction

It is difficult for students to change their habits and attitudes towards monitoring their own learning if self assessment is introduced towards the end of a course. However, it is also difficult for students entering from high school to change the habits acquired there. They have had many years of being socialized into expectations of authority-dependence and unilateral assessment by staff. It is at the early stages of a course, however, that students ideally ought to encounter the concept of self-assessment if it is to be taken seriously and applied effectively. Notwithstanding the problems of transition from school, the introduction should be made at the earliest possible stage, and the skills practised thereafter, most desirably in a sequence of courses through the years of a programme.

Similarly, within a particular subject, students should know what is expected of them at the beginning and should not have the idea of self assessment introduced once they have already developed an expectation of what is to occur in the course. There are always competing demands in the timetable and it is quite difficult to make room for new content or for a new approach. However, many successful self assessment exercises have been built around an existing activity in a course (an examination, or a class exercise) through making variations in the process (as in the Case Studies).

Enlisting student cooperation: incentives

One might hope that in a setting where there were no formal assessment constraints students would acknowledge the value of monitoring their own learning and willingly undertake it. However, it is sometimes necessary to offer some sort of incentive.

There are three options: making these incentives intrinsic to the task, making them extrinsic, or combining elements of the two. Incentives could include:
- appealing to pure intellectual curiosity,
- persuading students of the interest and value of the exercise,
- awarding marks for self assessment,
- building it in as a course requirement,
- allocation of class time or substitution for other assignments, rather than expecting students to take it as an extra task,
- or, using it for contracting for a grade.

In an ideal context it may be sufficient to appeal to students' best interests. But in many institutions it is necessary for staff to demonstrate their belief in the value of self assessment in a tangible fashion, by providing at least some extrinsic incentive.

CASE STUDY 4: Self assessment in an introductory engineering design class.

Teaching design is a complex matter in both engineering and architecture. It is a curriculum area demanding a high level of judgement on the part of students and requiring the development, in particular, of the high-level skills of synthesis. In light of the point we have made earlier, there would appear to exist a prima facie case for the introduction of self assessment from the earliest stage at which these sorts of studies are taken up.

The first design project experienced by mechanical engineering students at the University of New South Wales occurs in the second year of their course when they proceed through the stages of designing a pump according to certain specifications. A self assessment activity was linked to this project (Boud, Churches and Smith, 1986).

Prior to handing in their final design, students were given a self assessment schedule to complete, being supplied with criteria in the form of eleven factors relevant to good design and being asked to make an assessment of the extent to which they had been able to meet these criteria in their own project. They had the opportunity of suggesting further criteria, and they were also asked to complete an open-ended questionnaire which sought to elicit students views on the exercise.

Although these marks did not contribute to final assessment, 4% bonus marks were allocated for the conduct of the self assessment exercise. They were informed that these marks would be awarded on the basis of how skilfully they assessed their own work, on the amount of detail in their analysis and on the extent to which their assessment accurately reflected their actual performance.

In practice, however, it was not found possible for staff to make such fine discriminations as this plan would require. Hence marks were given to students who indicated a critical appreciation of the important design factors in their own design.

The study was conducted three years in succession with modifications to the procedure being made in the light of experience. Modifications mainly consisted of describing the design factors more precisely. The number of students who considered it a worthwhile learning experience was high (75%, 77% and 72% respectively) and negative responses focussed on the additional load caused by self assessment in an already overloaded course. In the light of these responses consideration is being given to introducing self assessment activities into all years of mechanical engineering design.

Communication and conflict

As self assessment may be quite a novel idea in some courses it can be useful to give students an opportunity to discuss it fully and allow them to influence the way in which it is used. Such negotiation can lead to more effective implementation, but staff need to avoid being drawn into undesirable practices.

Two possible areas of conflict have become evident:
- It is quite common for students to wish to use time spent or effort expended as criteria for judging their work, and this is generally not acceptable to staff.
- Conversely, staff assessing students' work often use criteria which they have not revealed to them and which they may not have acknowledged to themselves that they are using.

The solution to both problems lies in explicit communication. It is desirable, as a general rule, for both staff and students to be quite explicit about their criteria and their judgements. Only in this way can these be kept open to critical scrutiny, and only thus can students learn to appreciate the full range of considerations which are relevant to work of the kind in which they are engaged.

Criteria for judging performance

One of the most difficult aspects of self assessment for students, and necessarily for staff, is thinking in terms of criteria. Very often staff have a notion of what are the standards they should apply to a particular kind of work, for example an essay, but they have difficulties in articulating them. They know what is good when they see it, but they find it hard to describe it to others. This is an issue which goes to the heart of teaching in higher education: if teachers are unable to clearly specify their standards for good work, how can students learn to produce it? Dealing with tacit knowledge takes us far beyond the scope of this Guide, but it is important for staff to be as clear as possible about what criteria are, and what would constitute satisfactory criteria.

1.   Clarifying the concept of assessment criteria

In all cases it is necessary for the concept of criteria for assessment to be presented in operational terms with which all participants are familiar. This may take the form of asking:
    'how would you distinguish good from poor work in this subject?'
    or
    'what would be the factors which characterised a good assignment in this course?'.

It is not desirable to ask students to guess what criteria their teachers would use as this may personalise the issue and may discourage students thinking for themselves.

2.   The elements of satisfactory criteria

Criteria should include information about:
    • the area to be assessed,
    • the aims to be pursued, and
    • the standards to be reached.

Moreover, these should all be spelled out at such a level of detail as will make it possible for the person making the judgement to know the extent to which the criteria have been met.

The above represents an ideal case, however, and in practice rather less than this may be adequate under circumstances where it can be demonstrated that the appropriate standards in the given subject can be applied without them being stated explicitly.

Strategies for generating criteria

Although the objective is for students to reach their own decisions about criteria for assessing themselves, and hopefully about how they arrive at such criteria, it is important to understand the facilitative role the teacher plays in this process. Two techniques which can be used for this purpose are structured written schedules for developing individual criteria and structured group activities for reaching consensus on common criteria.

1.   Structured written schedules

These have been found most useful when used as a basis for self assessment by individual students (as distinct from a class group). Basically they consist of a list of written instructions to guide each student through a sequence of steps involving:

- identifying the criteria which they consider appropriate to apply to their work,
- clarifying these criteria, and
- assessing the priority or emphasis which they wish to give to each.

These steps consist of questions which are as easy to complete as possible; a starting point might be:

1. List the factors you would take into account in assessing your assignment.
2. List the factors you would take into account when assessing another person's assignment.
3. Look through each list carefully and decide if you could recognise each item in the work of someone else. Rewrite any item in your list that you could not recognise in someone's work.
4. Reread your list. Could each item be readily understood by someone else without explanation? Rewrite any ambiguous statements.
5. Decide what priority you would place on each item. Number them in order of importance.
   (adapted from Boud and Tyree 1980)

Once satisfactory criteria have been generated in this way, students then use them as the yardsticks by which they judge their own performance. In some cases this will consist simply of:
- awarding themselves a mark with respect to each criterion, and then
- making a statement justifying that mark.

Alternatively, they may simply make a statement indicating the extent to which they have satisfied each criterion. Case Study 5 exemplifies these strategies.

CASE STUDY 5:   Self and peer assessment of class participation in law

A characteristic of teaching in the University of New South Wales School of Law is the emphasis placed on the contribution of class participation in student assessment. This normally comprised 20% of the final marks for each subject.

This assessment of class participation had been regarded by staff as one of the more contentious aspects of the assessment system and there was much discussion about the appropriate procedures to be used (Armstrong and Boud 1983). It was therefore decided to investigate the possibilities of using self and peer assessment to generate the class participation grade. A study was mounted in a first year class of 25 students on 'The Legal system' (Boud and Tyree 1980).

One of the appealing features of implementing self and peer assessment in this particular context is that unlike the case of examinations – students' class participation is a directly observable phenomenon. All students in the class have direct access to it without additional study of materials or the devotion of extra time over and above time spent in normal class discussions.

Instructions were provided for each student, giving guidelines for constructing assessment criteria. These also focussed students' attention on the need to establish priorities and the need for criteria to be clearly written.

Once students had individually identified the criteria they were going to adopt, they then used the top three of these, to make an assessment of both their own performance in the class and that of the other students. All students therefore judged the performance of themselves and their peers according to a unique set of criteria which they had each developed as individuals. Students also responded to a questionnaire which aimed to elicit their views of the self and peer assessment process. Marks generated were not used as part of formal assessment.

Each student contributed between 5 and 8 criteria, all of which were considered by staff to be valid ones.

The main findings of this study were that:
  (a)   there was a very high level of agreement between the average of the marks given by peers and those given by the teacher,
  (b)   students tended to rate themselves more favourably than they were rated by their peers,
  (c)   students tended to rate themselves less favourably than they were rated by their teacher.

(d)   It was also observed that student reaction was very positive, especially to the criteria-setting part of the exercise.

---

2.   Structured group activities

These would be used when it is desired to generate common criteria for a class, as is frequently the case when students enrolled in a particular subject are expected to be assessed using identical criteria. It is the common, familiar approach used by teachers in making assessment of students in class.

If students are to be involved in generating these criteria for purposes of self or peer assessment, it becomes necessary to find ways in which they can – as a group – identify, discuss and agree upon a common set of them. One method which has been found particularly useful is based upon the nominal group technique (Delbecq, Van der Ven and Gustafson 1975). The word nominal is used as the group functions as a group in name only and the interactions between members are restricted by certain rules. The following is one way (used in Case Study 2) of using that technique for generating self and peer assessment criteria.

(a)   Students are briefed in advance of the meeting that they will be expected to produce a number of criteria, say three, which will be considered by the class as a whole. To assist them at this stage they may be given a handout which gives them some guidance on how criteria for assessment might be phrased and what will happen in the meeting.

(b)   The meeting itself might be conducted by either the teacher or a colleague who is experienced in the use of nominal group methods. If the teacher leads the session it is particularly important that he or she be nonjudgemental about the criteria which are generated during the process and resist indicating either verbally or nonverbally their own thoughts about the criteria which are being discussed. The reason for this is that students may be inhibited from presenting their own responses when they hear teachers expressing their own opinions or values. If the teacher feels that it is not possible to maintain this role, then these are grounds for bringing in someone else who can be a neutral facilitator.

(c)   The leader of the session invites each person in turn to read out *one* of the criteria from their prepared list. This is written on a large sheet of paper where it can be seen by everyone. The criteria are listed until all have been recorded. Chalkboards, unless very large, or overhead projectors cannot be used as it is not possible to display all the criteria which are normally generated. Once all the criteria have been listed there is a period for clarification and for combining statements covering the same ground. Participants may be asked to suggest headings under which the criteria may be grouped. At this stage a straw vote may be taken on whether the criteria are acceptable. Students may agree to use the complete list, or to rate and choose the high priority items.

Making judgements

Making decisions about performance is considerably eased if there are explicit and unambiguous criteria. However, it is still a challenge for students to take their own work and make judgements about it. They can be assisted by devices which help them gain perspective on their work and which involve other people.

One way of gaining perspective is for students to apply the criteria to work to which they are not personally committed. For example, this could be a sample which the teacher provides which exhibits some of the features which are to be sought or to be avoided, or it could be the work of someone else in the same class. It can apply to students' own work if it has been completed at a much earlier date, but such delayed assessment can rarely be scheduled.

The contribution of other students can be a very useful input into the self assessment process. They have an opportunity to observe their peers throughout the learning process and often have a more detailed knowledge of the work of others than do their teachers. Students have been unwilling to make formal assessments of their peers in a number of cases known to the author. Reactions have been most positive when students have given specific feedback of a descriptive nature for the benefit of their peers and no grading has taken place. Thus, peer assessment serves to inform self assessment.

The main characteristics of this form of peer assessment are described in the document *Giving and Receiving Feedback: A Guide to the Use of Peers in Self Assessment* (see Appendix). Essentially, the desirable characteristics of peer feedback are no different from those of any other type of feedback from others, including that from teachers. In general such feedback should be specific, descriptive, predominantly non-judgemental in tone and form, directed towards the goals of the person receiving it and well timed. It should also refer to the particular work under consideration and not to attributes of the person which were not manifested in that work. It is also normally necessary for students to be given, or for them to establish, clear guidelines on what is being assessed and the form of the assessment activity.

One of the practical constraints on using peer feedback in courses is the amount of time required for students to gain sufficient appreciation of each others' work to enable valid comments to be made. It is particularly important for students to have time to examine and think about the work on which they are giving feedback, otherwise their comments may be superficial. This implies that, except in very small classes (perhaps of less than six students), it is not possible for a student to get feedback from all other students in the class even if this was thought desirable.

Realistically, it is unlikely that one person can give detailed and useful feedback under normal time constraints to more than three or four others. The extent to which this is possible also depends on the complexity of the work and the degree to which it is publicly available for discussion and comparison. It is easier to engage in peer feedback in a design class when drawings and sketches are displayed than it is in a subject which normally requires the production of essays. Even so, students are not used to commenting on the work of others. They therefore need more time than staff to do this both in order to appreciate the criteria which they are using and to formulate their responses in a useful form.

Once students have gained some distance from their work and perhaps received feedback from others, they are then in a position to make their own judgements using the criteria which they have earlier identified. It is quite common for additional criteria to become apparent at this stage, so it is necessary for the procedures which are adopted to be sufficiently flexible for these to be accommodated. One form of self assessment involves individuals making a judgement in a small group setting and then seeking feedback from peers prior to arriving at a final assessment (see Boud and Kilty 1985 for details). However, a supportive and mature group is needed for this to be effective.

Implications for Those Who Teach

If self assessment is to be introduced, with what matters should teachers concern themselves? In the light of the recent studies in Australian universities it is possible to identify some issues which should be considered.

The question of commitment

It is important, on both theoretical and empirical grounds, that staff embark on schemes to develop student self assessment procedures only when they themselves understand and become to some degree committed to the values which underpin this whole area. These values are contained in the premises above, and include principally the encouragement of student autonomy in learning and student responsibility for critical evaluation of their own work.

On the other hand there is empirical evidence that staff who may be at present not fully committed, or relatively neutral about the values involved, may nevertheless find it feasible to engage in small self assessment projects with their students. They might do this as a means of exploring the potential of the strategies and testing out their own response to the new values and ideas.

Institutional climate

The introduction of self assessment practices in the existing climate in many tertiary institutions can have the effect of raising quite profound questions about:
- the role of courses in higher education: are they to inculcate knowledge, develop students' intellectual skills, or what?,
- the educational purposes of professional courses: are they simply pre-service training or do they have a broader educational purpose?,
- the ways in which they are organised: if students are expected to take responsibility for their learning, why is this discouraged in practice?,
- and the validity of the assessment procedures associated with them: why is the development of self-assessment skills not an integral part of all assessment practices?

Considerations of questions such as these sometimes leads to changes in parts of the curriculum or in formal assessment practices, or at least pressure to review courses.

Practical problems

(a)   At the course level

It is tempting to think that the introduction of self assessment into a course might address some of its existing problems. This is rarely the case: on the contrary, it is very important to appreciate that the introduction of self assessment by itself cannot bring significant benefits if a course already stands in need of revision of teaching methods or teacher-based assessment procedures.

A particular issue which arises in the introduction of any new assessment procedure is that quite small variations in the approach adopted can produce very different responses from students. These should be anticipated and adaptations, often appearing to be quite small, need to be made. For example, instructions need to be explicit and unambiguous and specific details need to be given about what students should do. Asking students to list the level of performance required in particular aspects of an assignment and asking them to make a judgement about each one is normally more effective than simply requiring them to give an unjustified rating of factors they wish to take into account on a common scale.

(b)   At the individual level

Some staff teaching in professional courses tend to see themselves as chiefly responsible for the inculcation of the knowledge and practices of the discipline or profession. The result is that in teaching they focus almost exclusively on the formal content of the subject. This in turn leads to:

- inadequate consideration of the attitudes and needs of students
- neglect of the second order skills (e.g. learning how to learn) which are required for both learning and for professional practice.

In sum, the ways staff conceptualise their role as teachers, and the attitudes they hold towards this job, might not in all cases match closely enough the conditions necessary for effective implementation of student self-assessment.

Some Issues To Be Faced

To count or not to count?

One of the most difficult decisions to make in the design of self assessment procedures concerns whether marks should be generated which contribute towards a student's final mark in a subject. Insufficient research has been conducted on self assessment for grading purposes in real settings to enable conclusions to be reached about the effects of grading on students' self assessments or related issues. Implications for grading of the use of self assessment are however discussed in Boud (1989). Undoubtedly, when students' self-generated grades are to be formally recorded there is an extrinsic incentive for them to be over generous to themselves and to distort their self assessments. However, in a study which throws some light on this issue (Case Study 1), the size of the effect appeared to be very small, although the structure of the study may have contributed to this finding by deliberately minimising the scope for inflated marks.

It is not possible to conduct research studies on the effects of self marking which counts towards credit without either deceiving students as to the outcomes, or actually allowing the results to contribute towards their final assessment, thus, potentially disadvantaging students. If self assessment is treated in terms of students' ability to guess the grades they will receive from teachers, no doubt research studies could be simplified, but some of the most important aspects of self assessment such as self monitoring and the developing of the basic learning skills which are needed in any study context might be obscured.

Whether grades derived from self assessment should be used as a component of formal assessment in a subject needs to be decided on the basis of professional judgement in a given setting. One approach to this problem is for the teacher to make an independent grading which is compared with the self grading (Boud, forthcoming). When the two marks are within 10% or within the same grade band, the student receives his or her own mark. If there is a discrepancy greater than this both parties are required to present a justification of their grade to each other and agree on a suitable mark. If the parties are unable to agree, there is provision for all the evidence to be submitted to a third party who is free to make his or her own assessment unconstrained by the previous ones. The final step has not yet been required in eight years of use.

The use of self assessment in student grading is discussed more fully in Boud (1989). Situations in which the use of grading by students may be legitimate are summarised there as follows. "When:
  (a)   there is a high trust, high integrity learning environment;
  (b)   students are rewarded for high integrity marking;
  (c)   marks are moderated by staff so that deviations from staff marks need to be justified;
  (d)   blind peer marking is used as a check;
  (e)   random staff marking is used as a check;
  (f)   a major goal is the achievement of effective self assessment and students have had ample opportunity to practice and develop their skills;

(g)   the criteria against which achievement is to be judged have
       been sufficiently unambiguously defined for there to be
       little scope for misinterpretation of grade boundaries;
(h)   effort is explicitly excluded as a criterion."

The 'one-off' exercise and the need for practice

It is relatively easy to introduce a self assessment activity as a one-off
class exercise. suitable activities can be designed for a one hour
tutorial period which staff and students will find beneficial both in
terms of dealing with the substantive subject-matter of the course and
in terms of helping students think more clearly about what they are
studying.

While this is a valid application of the concept of self assessment and
can be a good starting point for its introduction, it remains true that
if the skills of assessing one's own work are to be developed and
integrated into students' normal learning patterns, then a more
systematic approach will need to be taken.

On a number of occasions in research studies staff have been surprised
by students' lack of insight into their own work and their poor
appreciation of the standards which staff have thought should apply.
There have, it should be noted, also been striking instances of the
converse. The source of this problem has been attributed in part to
students' lack of practice in making such assessments. In those
instances in which self assessment has become a regular and familiar
activity, no reports of this nature have been received.

Like any other complex academic skill, self assessment must be
practised if it is to be developed. It is not reasonable to expect that a
few isolated occurrences in one or two courses in an entire degree
programme will lead to a very substantial increase in students' ability
in this area. These may have the effect of stressing the importance of
skills in this area and may raise awareness about their cultivation, but
this alone does not count as skill development and, if ineptly
introduced, the result may be quite the opposite of what is desired.

Self assessment as a central feature of courses

Most of the discussion in this Guide has referred to examples of
student self assessment which were adjuncts to the main activities.
However, this need not always be the case; courses can have self
assessment as a central feature. This is easiest to achieve in courses
where there is a great emphasis on student autonomy. Cowan (1988)
gives a moving example of his struggles in doing this in an

undergraduate civil engineering course. As a final example here, Case Study 6 presents the use of self assessment in a course which has few of the normal constraints of class size and overstuffed curriculum. It shows how self assessment with peer feedback can be closely linked with major learning goals.

CASE STUDY 6   The use of self assessment
                      schedules in negotiated learning.

Postgraduate courses often place much greater emphasis on taking account of students' experience than undergraduate teaching. Outcomes from courses which link closely to professional practice are significantly influenced by the needs of participants. The author has been teaching in this context for the past thirteen years and developing an approach to the design and conduct of courses which builds upon students' experience and involves them in the planning of the curriculum and the conduct of classes (Boud and Prosser 1980).

The main question which arises for assessment in this context is what form of assessment is suitable when learning is negotiated, students have a very high degree of responsibility for their own learning and learning covers a wide range of matters not all of which are accessible to the staff member. One solution takes the form of the preparation of a self assessment schedule in which students summarise their learning and make judgements about their achievements and future plans (Boud, forthcoming).

The schedule is a document typically in the range of 2,000 to 4,000 words which students prepare towards the end of their course. It is constructed around the following headings:

Goals
Including both those goals identified at the beginning of the course and those which emerged during it.

Criteria
The yardsticks against which it is possible to judge whether the goals were achieved.

Evidence
Evidence of the pursuit and attainment of goals. Items might include reference to papers written, notes on readings, extracts from learning portfolios and accounts of work within their peer group.

Judgements
Self judgements, including those based upon reports of what others have said, qualitative analyses of the extent to which objectives had been met, and comments about the appropriateness of the criteria which have been used.

Further action
Further action contemplated to pursue the goals further, including the identification of new goals.

Students reflect on their learning and, using records which they have prepared during the course, document and analyse their achievements. Feedback from peers is useful and has been used prior to and during the preparation of such documents.

Self assessment schedules can either be used as the principal assessment task or in conjunction with assignments or specific projects. In the latter case, it can be combined with class-generated checklists of criteria for these specific tasks as described in Case Study 2.

Conclusion

The introduction of self assessment practices into existing courses is both feasible and practicable in courses of many different kinds and in a variety of circumstances. The case studies demonstrate how the process has been implemented successfully by practitioners in classes of widely different size and subject matter. However, it is important to stress that the form of self assessment needs to be appropriate to the setting. Although the use of self assessment may challenge some of the existing assumptions about current teaching and learning it is possible to start to develop the skills needed without dismantling existing structures.

Acknowledgements
I would like to thank all of those with whom I have collaborated in studies on self assessment. In particular I wish to acknowledge the support of Jackie Lublin, my co-investigator on an ERDC funded project on self assessment in professional education, and the helpful editorial advice of Lee Andresen, Peggy Nightingale and the anonymous Green Guide reviewers.

References

Armstrong, M.T. and Boud, D.J. (1983) Assessing class participation: an exploration of the issues, *Studies in Higher Education*, 8, 1, 33-44.

Boud, D.J. (1981) Independence and interdependence in distance education: responsive course design, *Aspects of Educational Technology*, 15, 55-60.

Boud, D.J. (1989) The role of self assessment in student grading, *Assessment and Evaluation in Higher Education*, 14, 1, 20-30

Boud, D.J. (forthcoming) The use of self assessment schedules in negotiated learning, *Studies in Higher Education*, 17, 2.

Boud, D.J., Churches, A. and Smith, E. (1986) Student self assessment in an engineering design course: an evaluation, *International Journal of Applied Engineering Education*, 2, 2, 83-90

Boud, D.J. and Falchikov, N. (1989) Quantitative studies of student self-assessment in higher education: a critical analysis of findings, *Higher Education*, 18, 5, 529-549

Boud, D.J. and Holmes, W.H. (1981) Self and peer marking in an undergraduate engineering course, *IEEE Transactions on Education*, E-24, 4, 267-274.

Boud, D.J. and Kilty, J.M. (1985) Self-appraisal: an approach to academic staff development, in Cryer, P. (ed) *Training Activities for Teachers in Higher Education, Volume Two*, Guildford: SRHE and NFER-Nelson, 33-44.

Boud, D.J. and Lublin, J. (1983) Student self assessment: educational benefits within existing resources, in Squires, G. (ed) *Innovation through Recession*, Guildford, Surrey: Society for Research into Higher Education, 93-99.

Boud, D.J. and Prosser, M.T. (1980) Sharing responsibility: staff-student cooperation in learning, *British Journal of Educational Technology*, 11, 1, 24-35 and also reprinted in Knowles, M.S. and Associates (1985) *Andragogy in Action*, San Francisco: Jossey-Bass, 175-188.

Boud, D.J. and Tyree, A.L. (1980) Self and peer assessment in professional education: a preliminary study in law, *Journal of the Society of Public Teachers of Law*, 15, 1, 65-74.

Delbecq, A., Van der Ven, A.M. and Gustafson, D.H. (1975) *Group Processes for Program Planning: A Guide to Nominal Group and Delphi Processes*, Glenview, Illinois: Scott Foreman

Falchikov, N. and Boud, D.J. (1989) Student self-assessment in higher education: a meta-analysis, *Review of Educational Research*, 59, 4, 395-430

Gale, J. (1984) Self-assessment and self-remediation strategies, in Henderson, E.S. and Nathenson, M.B. (eds) *Independent Learning in Higher Education*, Englewood Cliffs, New Jersey: Educational Technology Publications, 99-140.

Heron, J. (1981) Self and peer assessment, in Boydell, T. and Pedler, M. (eds) *Management Self-development: Concepts and Practices*, Westmead, Farnborough: Gower, 111-128.

Heron, J. (1988) Assessment revisited, in Boud, D.J. (ed) *Developing Student Autonomy in Learning*, Second Edition. London: Kogan Page, 77-90

Midgley, D.F. and Petty, M. (1983) *Final Report on the Alumni Association 1982 Survey of Graduate Opinions on General Education*, University of New South Wales Alumni Association, Kensington.

Appendix

Giving and Receiving Feedback:
A Guide to the Use of Peers in Self Assessment

Introduction

One of the most valuable contributions anyone can make to another person's learning is constructive comment. Whether as a student or as a teacher each one of us has the capacity to provide useful information to other people which will help them to learn more effectively.

To bother to give another person positive suggestions about their work indicates both that you care enough about them to spend your time considering their work and that their work is worthy of your attention. You are both affirming the worth of the person and offering them your views on something into which they have put some effort.

Everyone has the capacity for giving useful feedback and some people use it to more effect than others. The skills of giving and receiving feedback can be developed if attention is given to some of the attributes of worthwhile feedback and how it can be given so that its contribution to learning can be enhanced.

Good and Bad Feedback

Before looking in detail at useful feedback it is important to distinguish it from those types of feedback which can be unhelpful and sometimes positively harmful.

We all know what it is like to be on the receiving end of bad feedback: we feel 'got at', 'attacked', 'put down', 'damned' and generally invalidated as a person. some of the basic characteristics of bad feedback are that it is directed globally at the person; it is unhelpful, that is, it does not suggest what otherwise might be; it is ill-judged, it comes from the needs of the critic rather than the needs of the person receiving it; and it can provide a weight of destructive comment from which it is difficult for a person to surface: it is dehumanizing.

Useful feedback, on the other hand, affirms the worth of the person and gives support whilst offering reactions to the object of attention. Thus the person providing the feedback shows that he or she values the person who is receiving it and that the provider is sensitive to their needs and goals. This does not mean that only praise should be given, but that any critical matters should be raised in an overall supportive context in which the parties can trust one another.

Offering Feedback

In the discussion below the term 'work' or 'contribution' is used to describe the matter on which feedback is given. This 'work' may be of any type: an essay, a class contribution, a design, a project in any form: written, oral, graphic, etc.

There are many characteristics of worthwhile feedback but the most important is the way in which it is given. The tone, the style and the content should be consistent and provide the constant message: 'I appreciate you and what you have done and whatever else I say should be taken in this context". If you wish to give helpful feedback, you should:

Be realistic
- direct your comments towards matters about which the person can do something. Don't make suggestions which are entirely outside the scope of the matters at hand.

Be specific
- generalizations are particularly unhelpful. The person should be given sufficient information to pinpoint the areas to which you are referring and have a clear idea of what is being said about those *specific* areas.

Be sensitive to the goals of the person
- Just because the other person's contributions have not met your goals doesn't necessarily imply that something is wrong. The person produced the work for a specific purpose and you should be aware of that purpose and give your views accordingly. This is not to say that you can't make comments from your own perspective but that you should be clear when you offer views in terms of your own goals and you should say that is what you are doing. Link your comments to their intentions; listen carefully to what they have to say.

Be prompt
- time your comments appropriately. It is no use offering feedback after the person receiving it has put the work aside and moved on to other things. Respond promptly when your feedback is requested: to be effective feedback must be well-timed.

Be descriptive
- describe your views. Don't say what you think the person should feel. Don't be emotionally manipulative: you are offering your considered, rational views which should have the characteristics described here; it is up to the other person to accept or reject them as he or she sees fit.

Be diligent
- check your response. Is it an accurate reflection of what you want to express? Have you perceived the contribution accurately. There is nothing more annoying than to receive criticism from someone who clearly hasn't bothered to pay attention to what you have done.

Be direct
- say what you mean. Don't wrap it up in circumlocution, fancy words or abstract language.

Be consciously non-judgemental
- offer your personal view, do not act as an authority even if you may be one elsewhere. Give your personal reactions and feelings rather than value-laden statements. One way of doing this is to use comments of the type "I feel ... when you ...".

Receiving Feedback

There is no point in asking others to give you feedback unless you are prepared to be open to it and to consider comments which differ from your own perceptions. As receiver:

Be explicit
- make it clear what kind of feedback you are seeking. If necessary indicate what kinds you do not want to receive. The feedback from others is entirely for your benefit and if you do not indicate what you want you are unlikely to get it.

Be aware
- notice your own reactions, both intellectual and emotional. Particularly notice any reactions of rejection or censorship on your part. If the viewpoint from which the other is speaking is at variance with your own do not dismiss it: it can be important to realise the misapprehensions of others. Some people find it useful to partially dissociate or distance themselves in this situation and act as if they were witnessing feedback being given to someone else.

Be silent
- refrain from making a response. Don't even begin to frame a response in your own mind until you have listened carefully to what has been said and have considered the implications. Don't be distracted by the need to explain: if you really need to give an explanation do it later after the feedback session.

Written versus face-to-face feedback

There is no difference in principle between feedback given in written form and that in person. However, with written feedback there is normally no opportunity to resolve misunderstandings and it is necessary to be very explicit in specifying what types of feedback are desired and in formulating responses. In the written form more attention needs to be given to tone and style than would usually be the case in person.